# SIMPSONS™ COMICS

# GET SOME FANCY BOOK LEARNIN'

TITAN BOOKS

D1077497

**SIMPSONS COMICS
GET SOME FANCY BOOK LEARNIN'**

Collects Simpsons Comics 62, 70, 76, 126 and 148

Copyright © 2001, 2002, 2006, 2008, and 2010 by
Bongo Entertainment, Inc. All rights reserved.
No part of this book may be used or reproduced in any manner whatsoever
without written permission except in the case of brief quotations
embodied in critical articles and reviews. For information address
Bongo Comics Group c/o Titan Books
P.O. Box 1963, Santa Monica, CA 90406-1963

Published in the UK by Titan Books, a division of Titan Publishing Group Ltd.,
144 Southwark St., London SE1 0UP, under licence from Bongo Entertainment, Inc.

FIRST EDITION: FEBRUARY 2010

ISBN 9781848565197

2 4 6 8 10 9 7 5 3 1

Publisher: Matt Groening
Creative Director: Bill Morrison
Managing Editor: Terry Delegeane
Director of Operations: Robert Zaugh
Art Director: Nathan Kane
Art Director Special Projects: Serban Cristescu
Production Manager: Christopher Ungar
Assistant Art Director: Chia-Hsien Jason Ho
Production/Design: Karen Bates, Nathan Hamill, Art Villanueva
Staff Artist: Mike Rote
Administration: Ruth Waytz, Pete Benson
Intern: Max Davison
Legal Guardian: Susan A. Grode

Trade Paperback Concepts and Design: Serban Cristescu

Contributing Artists:
Karen Bates, John Costanza, Serban Cristescu, Dan Davis, Mike DeCarlo,
Luis Escobar, Jason Ho, Nathan Kane, Carol Lay, Joey Mason, Bill Morrison, Kevin M. Newman,
Phyllis Novin, Phil Ortiz, Howard Shum, Steve Steere Jr., Art Villanueva

Contributing Writers:
Ian Boothby, Carol Lay, Linda Medley, Sherri L. Smith

PRINTED IN CANADA

# CONTENTS

# GREEK MYTHS

HOMER, WE DON'T WANT TO HEAR ABOUT "THE ILIAD" ANYMORE.

OKAY, NO PROBLEMO. ONCE UPON...

OR "THE ODYSSEY."

GIVE US A *GOOD* STORY, OR WE'LL TELL EVERYONE YOU'RE *NOT REALLY BLIND.*

AAAAH! *DON'T DO THAT!*

THE ONLY WAY I COULD GET THIS *CUSHY STORYTELLING JOB* IS BY *PRETENDING* TO BE BLIND.

OTHERWISE IT'S BACK TO BEING A *SLAVE* IN THE *OLIVE MINES.*

THWAK!

I GOT THE IDEA OF *FAKING* BLIND-NESS FROM MY PAL OEDIPUS.

YOU WOULDN'T BELIEVE THE STORY *I* HAD TO MAKE UP.

OKAY, HERE'S A *NEW ONE* FOR YOU. ONCE THERE WERE THESE *THREE ROOMMATES*, ONE NAMED JACK, ONE NAMED JANET, AND ONE NAMED CHRISSY. BUT WHAT THEIR *LAND-LORD* MR. ROPER DIDN'T KNOW WAS...

TELL US A STORY ABOUT *THE GODS.*

THE GODS, EH?

OKAY...

# THE GODS in LABOR PAINS

ONCE UPON A TIME THERE WAS A KING OF THE GODS NAMED *ZEUS* WHO WAS *LOVED* BY ONE AND ALL.

Mount Olympus
A GATED COMMUNITY

ZEUS!

AHHHH!

LIGHTNING BOLTS

OOPS! MY LIGHTNING BOLTS FELL TO EARTH! WELL, THERE GOES SODOM AND GOMORRAH.

I'LL GET THE *NEW GUY* TO TAKE THE HEAT FOR IT.

OH, GOD, IT BURNS!

ZEUS, DID YOU TURN INTO A *SWAN* LAST NIGHT AND GO TO THE *SINGLES BAR?*

NO!

THEN WHAT'S WITH ALL THE *FEATHERS* AND THAT *EGG* YOU LAID?

OKAY, OKAY! I DID A BIT OF *HARM-LESS FLIRTING*. BUT YOU KNOW ME, HERA, IT *NEVER* GOES *FARTHER* THAN THAT.

HEY, DAD! IT'S ME, HERCULES, YOUR *ILLEGITIMATE SON!*

*WAP!*

D'OH!

HAVE YOU NO *SHAME?*

I'M A *DEMI-GOD* AND PROUD OF IT, MAN.

NOW WHAT IS THERE TO DO AROUND THIS PLACE? THINK I'M GONNA *CRASH* FOR A WHILE.

OH, *I'LL* FIND YOU SOMETHING TO DO.

LATER THAT DAY...

*TWELVE LABORS.* AW, MAN! *LABORS* ARE WORSE THAN *CHORES!*

HEY, YOU THINK *YOU* GOT IT *TOUGH?* WHEN *I* WAS YOUR AGE, MY DAD *ATE* ME.

CAN I COME BACK HOME NOW?

NO! I CAN STILL SMELL *ME* ON YOUR BREATH.

CONSARN IT!

IT'S NOT FAIR. NONE OF THE OTHER KIDS HAVE TO *FIGHT MONSTERS.*

LATER...

WELL, THAT TOOK A WHILE, BUT THEY'RE ALL CAUGHT.

DADDY! I WANT TO *ADOPT* THE MINOTAUR.

NOW REMEMBER THIS CAN'T BE LIKE THE GRYPHON OR THE SPHINX. YOU HAVE TO FEED IT AND CHANGE THE LITTER BOX EVERY DAY.

YOU ONLY DID *TEN* OUT OF THE *TWELVE LABORS!*

LISTEN LADY, TEN OUT OF TWELVE IS A B+ AND THAT'S THE *BEST GRADE* I EVER GOT!

HRMMM...

HEY, WHAT'S *WRONG?*

OH, IT'S ZEUS! HE'S AT THE BAR AGAIN, AND I HAVE TO DO EVERYTHING.

YOU LOOK GOOD IN THAT CHAIR. MAYBE *YOU* SHOULD BE THE ONE *RUNNING THINGS.*

ME? NO, I...YOU *THINK?*

AND SO HERA *TOOK OVER* OLYMPUS, AND EVERYTHING WORKED OUT JUST FINE.

WELL, *ALMOST* EVERYTHING.

CLEAN YOUR ROOM!

DO YOUR HOMEWORK!

I SAID THERE'S A 9 P.M. CURFEW, AND *I MEANT IT!*

WAY TO GO JERK-ULES!

# "THE HADES YOU SAY"

THE CASE YOU ARE ABOUT TO SEE IS *REAL*. THE LITIGANTS ARE NOT *MORTALS*. THEY ARE *ACTUAL GODS* WHO HAVE AGREED TO HAVE THEIR *DISPUTE* SETTLED HERE IN OUR FORUM...

...ATHENA'S COURT.

YOU MAY BE SEATED.

I HAVE GOAT LEGS.

I'VE READ YOUR *COMPLAINTS*. PERSEPHONE, YOU CLAIM THAT HADES *KIDNAPPED* YOU.

YES, YOUR HONOR.

OH, HERE WE GO!

MR. HADES, I AM JUST GOING TO SAY THIS ONCE. FIRST, TALK ONLY WHEN I AM ASKING A QUESTION, AND SECOND...

...PUT YOUR SHIRT BACK ON AND TAKE YOUR FEET OFF THE PODIUM.

OKAY! OKAY!

SHEEESH! WHAT *IS* THIS, *CHURCH*?

MR. HADES, WHAT IS *YOUR* SIDE OF THE STORY?

WELL, YOU SEE YOUR HONOR...

"IT ALL STARTED LIKE ANY OTHER DAY."

AND STAY OFF!

HADES
IF YOU WERE DEAD YOU'D BE HOME BY NOW.

THAT GUY HAS GOT TO LEARN TO PAY HIS TAB!

HUH? YOU SAY SOMETHING, *CHARON*?

WHASSA MATTER, *HADES*? YOU LOOK *DEPRESSED*.

YOU GOT IT *ALL!* POWER! LOOKS! CORPSES COMING OUT THE WAZOO...!

I'M *LONELY*.

WHY DON'T YA GET YOURSELF A *WIFE*?

THAT SOUNDS LIKE A *JIM-DANDY* IDEA.

SHUT UP, *SISYPHUS!*

WELL, I JUST DROPPED BY TO TELL YOU THAT IT TOOK *FOREVER*, BUT I FINALLY GOT THAT ROCK UP TO THE TOP OF THE HILL LIKE YOU WANTED.

AW, FIDDLESTICKS!

HEH, HEH!

MAYBE YOU'RE RIGHT, CHARON. I'M GONNA TRY *DATING*.

"THEN, JUDGE, I SAW THIS REAL *PRETTY WOMAN* IN THE *LAND OF THE LIVING* AND THOUGHT I'D ASK HER OUT."

WHAT A NICE FLOWER!

CRAAAAAACK!

RUMBLE!

AAAAAH!

YOU SEE! THIS IS EXACTLY WHY I DON'T LIKE EATING OUTDOORS!

IS ALL THIS *TRUE*, MS. PERSEPHONE?

MY FLUTE'S STUCK.

IT IS, YOUR HONOR. I TOLD HIM IN *NO UNCERTAIN TERMS* HOW I FELT.

OW! WHAT WAS *THAT* FOR?

I WAS JUST ASKING YOU OUT.

YOU'VE GOT A LOT TO LEARN ABOUT DATING.

AND I WANT *YOU* TO TEACH ME.

WELL, I REALLY SHOULDN'T, BUT...

LET'S HAVE DINNER. JUST DINNER.

OKAY.

21

WELL, I GOTTA GO. I HAVE A *HOT DATE* TONIGHT.

HOPE IT WORKS OUT.

IF NOT, IT'S A *BLT* FOR BREAKFAST.

OKAY, PERSEUS, SHE'S ALONE. HOW *HARD* CAN IT BE TO CUT OFF SOMEONE'S HEAD? DRUNK BARBERS DO IT EVERY DAY.

I SEE YOU.

HA! I CAME PREPARED! I HAVE A *MIRROR!*

IT'S NOT MY *LOOK* THAT TURNS MEN TO STONE. IT'S MY *SECOND-HAND SMOKE!*

UM...I'M GONNA START RUNNING NOW.

I UNDER-STAND.

HISSSSSS!

AAAH!

GOTTA TRY PLAN B.

HAMSTERS *AWAY!*

YUM!

MMMM!

AW, C'MON GUYS, I JUST FED YOU!

AAAAA

LATER...

YOU'RE *ALIVE?!?!*

YES, AND I'VE *HONORED* MY SIDE OF OUR DEAL. I'VE BROUGHT THE HEAD OF MEDUSA.

:GASP!:

AND I'M THROW-ING IN THE BODY FOR *FREE*.

WHAT'S THE MEANING OF THIS?

MEDUSA TOLD ME THAT YOU TWO USED TO DATE UNTIL SHE DUMPED YOU.

HE'S NEVER REALLY *GOTTEN OVER* ME. THIS WAS JUST HIS WAY OF GETTING MY ATTENTION.

THAT'S RIDICULOUS. I...

I'VE NEVER FORGOTTEN YOU OR STOPPED CARING, YOU *CRUEL DICTATOR* YOU.

REALLY?

WILL YOU *MARRY ME* AND MAKE ME THE *HAPPIEST DESPOT* IN THE WORLD?

I WILL!

AND SO...

WHAT A WONDERFUL WEDDING. THE BRIDE LOOKS SO BEAUTIFUL.

AND HERE COMES THE GROOM.

YOU ALWAYS LOVED THE *STRONG SILENT TYPE*.

I COULDN'T BE HAPPIER. HE'S *MY ROCK*.

AND NOW IT'S TIME FOR *MY WEDDING GIFT*.

*DOVES*. HOW SWEET!

COO!

COO!

COO!

THEY WERE OUT OF DOVES, SO I GOT *PIGEONS* INSTEAD.

*PERSEUS!*

HEH, HEH!

25

AND SO, ALL THE HEROES, GODS, KINGS, AND GORGONS LIVED *HAPPILY EVER AFTER*. THE END!

HEY? WHERE'D EVERYBODY GO?

ARE *YOU* STILL HERE? WE STOPPED LISTENING TO *YOUR STORY* HOURS AGO.

THEN WHO ARE YOU...

AESOP?

SORRY, WE'RE FULL UP, SIR. BUT THERE'S SOME *STANDING ROOM TICKETS* LEFT FOR THE TEN O'CLOCK SHOW.

AND SO THE HARE LEARNED THAT EVEN THOUGH HE WAS *FASTER* THAN THE TORTOISE, SLOW AND STEADY WINS THE RACE.

LOUSY, NON-BLIND, STORYTELLING SLAVE TAKING MY BUSINESS!

I GUESS NO ONE *CARES* ABOUT THE GODS ANYMORE.

WHAM!

*TELL* ME ABOUT IT.

OH...AND BARKEEP? IF MY *WIFE* CALLS, I'M NOT HERE.

THE END

# AESOP'S FABLES

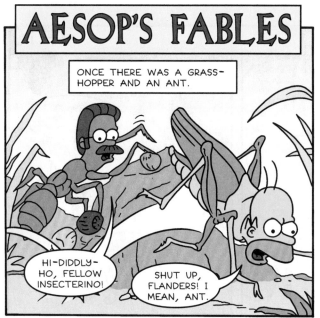

ONCE THERE WAS A GRASS-HOPPER AND AN ANT.

HI-DIDDLY-HO, FELLOW INSECTERINO!

SHUT UP, FLANDERS! I MEAN, ANT.

THE ANT *WORKED* HARD.

WHILE THE *LAZY* GRASS-HOPPER JUST DRANK BEER AND PLAYED HIS FIDDLE.

THE ANT SAID...

YOU REALLY SHOULD *PREPARE* FOR WINTER!

THE GRASSHOPPER REPLIED...

WHAT PART OF SHUT UP AREN'T YOUR ANTENNA RECEIVING?

THEN WINTER FINALLY CAME, AND THE ANT, WHO HAD WORKED HARD, HAD LOTS OF FOOD *STORED*, WHILE THE GRASSHOPPER HAD *NONE*.

HEY, ANT, CAN I HAVE *HALF* YOUR FOOD?

SURE.

THANKS.

GOSH-DIDDLY-DARN IT!

MORAL: WORKING IS FOR *SUCKERS*.

THERE ONCE WAS A FOX WHO SPOTTED SOME GRAPES.

YEAH! THAT'S WHAT I COULD GO FOR!

BUT THEY WERE *TOO HIGH* TO REACH.

GRRR! LOUSY STINKING GRAPES! I'LL GOUGE OUT YOUR PITS AND MAKE RAISINS OF YOUR CHILDREN!

AW, THEY'RE PROBABLY *SOUR*.

WOLF! WOLF!

HEY, I'M DOIN' A FABLE HERE!

A WOLF? WHERE?

OH, IT'S JUST A FOX!

HEY, NOW THAT YOU'RE HERE, HOW ABOUT GETTING ME THEM GRAPES?

YEAH, OKAY.

THESE AIN'T SOUR AT ALL. NOW HOW AM I GONNA MAKE *WINE* OUT OF 'EM?

IF YOU'RE NOT GOING TO EAT THOSE, CAN I HAVE THEM? THE ANT'S FOOD REALLY *STINKS*.

I CAN HEAR YOU, HOMER! I MEAN, GRASS-HOPPER!

WOLF! WOLF!

ACH! 'TIS JUST A WEE DOG.

WHAT'S WRONG?

I HAD A **WONDERFUL BONE**, BUT I SAW A DOG WITH ANOTHER ONE IN THE WATER, AND WHEN I TRIED TO BITE IT, I **LOST** MINE.

HOLY ZEUS! IT'S A **TALKING DOG!**

SO? YOU'RE A TALKING FOX.

HEY, YOU'RE RIGHT. THAT **IS** PRETTY COOL.

SPEAKING OF COOL, WHAT'S WITH THE **WEATHER,** MAN?

WE HAVE A **BET** GOING TO SEE WHO CAN MAKE YOU TAKE OFF YOUR JACKET **FIRST!**

¦COUGH!¦ ¦COUGH!¦ WE HAVE TEN DRACHMAS RIDING ON IT.

I'LL TAKE IT OFF FOR WHOEVER GIVES ME **FIVE DRACHMAS** FIRST.

WIND IT IS!

NO FAIR! SHE **BLEW** MY FIVE AWAY!

WHAT ARE YOU GONNA DO WITH THE MONEY?

PUT IT ALL ON THE *TORTOISE* TO WIN *THE BIG RACE!*

NO CHECKS

ARE YOU NUTS? THE ODDS ARE 300 TO 1!

AND THE WINNER IS... THE HARE!

SEE! I TOLD YA.

JUST WAIT.

MAY I HAVE YOUR ATTENTION PLEASE. AFTER A *RANDOM URINE TEST FOR STEROIDS,* THE HARE HAS BEEN *DISQUALIFIED.* THE TORTOISE *WINS.*

YES!

CONGRATULATIONS ON YER WIN, LAD!

YES, WELL DONE!

IT'S A WOLFMAN!

OH, NO, WE'RE NOT FALLING FOR *THAT* AGAIN!

NOT A WOLF, *MAN.* IT'S A *WOLFMAN!* AND THE MUMMY! AND DRACULA!

OH MY GODS! THEY'RE *ATTACKING* THE DANCING MONKEYS, THE JACKDAW, THE CRAB, AND IT'S MOTHER.

BUT HERE COME THE TWO FIGHTING COCKS AND THE EAGLE!

I'VE NE'ER SEEN SUCH AN *INCREDIBLE BATTLE* WITH SO MANY *INTERESTING LOOKIN' CHARACTERS!*

IT'D BE *RIDICULOUS* TO EVEN ASK ANY ARTIST TO TRY AND DRAW ALL THAT.

ZZZZAP! ZZZZAP!

AHHH! *FLYING SAUCERS!*

RUN FOR IT!

...AND THEN THE *ALIENS* FIRED THEIR *DEATH RAYS,* BUT WHAT THEY DIDN'T KNOW WAS THAT THE *MOLE PEOPLE* HAD PLANNED FOR THIS AND...

HOMER! WOULD YOU QUIT *INTERRUPTING* MY FABLES?

I WAS JUST TRYING TO *JAZZ THEM UP!* YOU'RE NOT PLAYING WELL IN THE *KEY 18-32 DEMOGRAPHIC.*

HE'S RIGHT, YOU KNOW. I'M AFRAID WE'RE GOING TO HAVE TO GIVE YOUR SPOT TO AN *INFOMERCIAL.*

BUT...

NOW, NOW! YOU CAN'T HAVE A *GREEK DEMOCRACY* WITHOUT DEMOGRAPHICS.

HI, EVERYBODY!

HI, HYPOCRATES!

HOW MUCH WOULD YOU PAY TO GET RID OF THAT ANNOYING SANDAL RASH?

MORAL? THE HADES IF I KNOW.

# LISA & MAGGIE SIMPSON in PANDORA, JR.

FRIDAY NIGHT "B" THERE FOR THE B-SHARPS!

HO! WHAT'S THIS?

AN ANCIENT *BOX!*

= SUCK SUCK =

MAYBE IT HOLDS *TREASURE!*

OR MAYBE IT HOLDS A *MUMMY'S HAND* THAT WILL CRAWL AROUND IN THE NIGHT LIKE A *SPIDER!*

*CAROL LAY*
SCRIPT & ART

*NATHAN KANE*
COLORS

*KAREN BATES*
LETTERS

*BILL MORRISON*
EDITOR

BACK IN ANCIENT TIMES, THE GOD *ZEUS* WAS MAD AT A MAN NAMED *EPIMETHEUS* FOR HELPING PROMETHEUS STEAL FIRE TO GIVE TO THE HUMANS. HE CREATED A BEAUTIFUL WIFE FOR EPIMETHEUS AND NAMED HER *PANDORA*.

YOU MAY KISS THE BRIDE.

"ZEUS WAS KIND OF MEAN, AND HE WANTED TO PLAY A TRICK ON HUMANITY."

HEH HEH HEH...

"SO HE GAVE PANDORA *CURIOSITY*, BUT HE ALSO GAVE HER AN ORNATE BOX AND SAID..."

YOU MUST *NEVER* OPEN THIS!

"THE GOOD WIFE STRUGGLED TO KEEP FROM OPENING THE BOX. AFTER ALL, THE BOSS OF THE GODS TOLD HER NEVER TO DO SO."

"BUT ONE DAY HER CURIOSITY WON OUT, AND SHE THOUGHT SHE MIGHT JUST TAKE A PEEK."

KREAKK...

"WHEN SHE DID SO, ALL KINDS OF DEMONS, DISEASE, AND SADNESS ESCAPED INTO THE WORLD."

"SHE TRIED TO SHUT THE BOX, BUT IT WAS TOO LATE."

"WHEN SHE LOOKED INSIDE, ALL THAT WAS LEFT WAS SMALL AND DELICATE."

"IT WAS *HOPE*."

SO SOMETIMES, LITTLE SISTER, SATISFYING CURIOSITY CAN LEAD TO MISERY.

-SUCK SUCK-

I HAVE AN IDEA! LET'S PRETEND I'M *ZEUS* AND YOU'RE *PANDORA*.

OK, PANDORA... DON'T OPEN THAT BOX.

*EVER*.

=SUCK SUCK=

LI-SA...!

COMING, MOM!

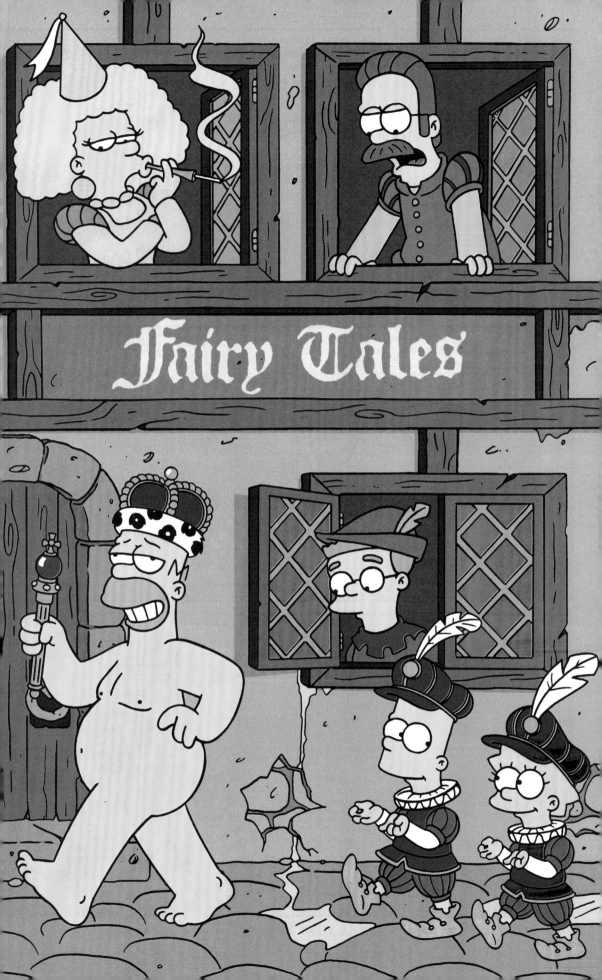

Fairy Tales

# HUMPTY DUMPED

## a Mother Marge tale

HUMPTY DUMPTY SAT ON A WALL.

I LIKE SITTING IN THE SUN. IT MAKES ME FEEL ALL *POACHY* INSIDE.

EL BARTO

POST NO BILLS

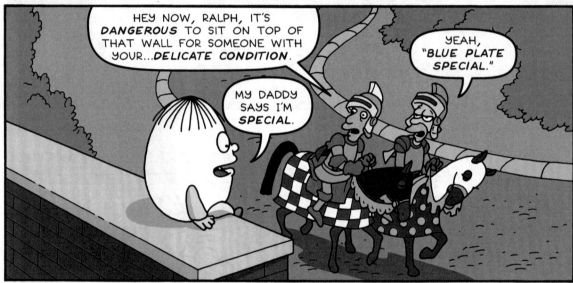

HEY NOW, RALPH, IT'S *DANGEROUS* TO SIT ON TOP OF THAT WALL FOR SOMEONE WITH YOUR...*DELICATE CONDITION.*

MY DADDY SAYS I'M *SPECIAL.*

YEAH, *"BLUE PLATE SPECIAL."*

IF I LEAN BACK, I CAN SEE GOD!

FOR CRYIN' OUT LOUD, AT LEAST STOP *ROCKING!*

THIS WON'T END WELL.

STORY: SHERRI SMITH • ART: JOHN COSTANZA / JASON HO • PRODUCTION: KAREN BATES / SERBAN CRISTESCU

# Hans Across America

**IAN BOOTHBY & LINDA MEDLEY-STORY**

| IAN BOOTHBY | JOHN COSTANZA | PHYLLIS NOVIN | ART VILLANUEVA | KAREN BATES | BILL MORRISON |
|---|---|---|---|---|---|
| SCRIPT | PENCILS | INKS | COLORS | LETTERS | EDITOR |

MATT GROENING

WELL, OKAY! BOYS, LISA'S GONNA READ YOU A STORY OR TWO!

YAY!

ONCE UPON A TIME, A MERMAID WAS HAVING HER EIGHTEENTH BIRTHDAY!

# The Little Mermaid

YOU KNOW, I DON'T REALLY NEED CANDLES.

CLICK!! CLICK!

GOOD, CAUSE THIS IS MURDER ON MY THUMB!

CONGRATS! YOU'RE NOW OLD ENOUGH TO SWIM TO THE SURFACE!

!GASP!! IS THAT SAFE?

SURE, WE DO IT ALL THE TIME!

IT'S REALLY HARD TO SMOKE UNDERWATER!

COME ON! WE'LL SHOW YOU!

THIS IS GONNA END BADLY!

WHY DO YOU ALWAYS HAVE TO BE SO NEGATIVE?

I'M A HERMIT CRAB. BEING AN ANTI-SOCIAL GRUMP IS WHAT I DO!

YOU WERE DROWNING AND NAKED, SO I MADE YOU THOSE!

NAKED? BUT LUIGI SAID HE MADE ME AN OUTFIT ONLY CLASSY PEOPLE COULD SEE!

SAY, THANKS FOR SAVING MY LIFE. WANNA GO OUT SOMETIME? A LITTLE DINNER AND DANCING?

DANCING? WELL, I...ER... THAT IS...

LOOK OVER THERE!

WHAT? WHO? WHERE? WHY?

HELLO?

LATER...

SO *THAT'S* MY PROBLEM. I NEED *LEGS* TO DANCE WITH THIS HANDSOME MAN!

CAN YOU HELP ME, SEA WITCH?

WHY DOES EVERYONE CALL ME "SEA WITCH"? MY NAME'S *AGNES*!

YOUR SON TOLD ME TO.

IT'S JUST A NICKNAME I HAVE FOR YOU, MOTHER. AN *AFFECTIONATE* NICKNAME!

HERE'S THE DEAL, TOOTS! I'LL GIVE YOU A PAIR OF GAMS, BUT I WANT YOUR TONGUE IN RETURN!

MY TONGUE?

YEAH, MINE'S NO GOOD. BURNED ALL MY TASTE BUDS OFF IN A HOT WING-EATING CONTEST!

LUCKILY, MERMAID TONGUES AND LOWER HALVES ARE DETACHABLE, SO THIS WAS PAINLESS...

MMMM...OH, AND ONE MORE THING I FORGOT TO TELL YOU.

IF YOUR TRUE LOVE MARRIES SOMEONE ELSE, YOU'LL TURN TO FOAM!

WHATSA MATTER, PRINCE HOMER?

I MET THE GIRL OF MY DREAMS TODAY, BUT SHE LEFT ME!

YOU'LL BOUNCE BACK. MAN, IF I WUZ A HANDSOME PRINCE LIKE YOU, I'D BE KISSING ALL THE PRINCESSES IN COMAS I COULD FIND, TRYING TO WAKE 'EM UP!

I DID THAT ONCE. I'M NOT ALLOWED AT THE HOSPITAL ANYMORE.

SQUEAK!

WOW, CHECK OUT THE LEGS ON *HER*!

THEY LOOK BRAND NEW!

≡GASP!≡ IT'S *YOU*!

45

WAIT! WAIT! BEFORE YOU SAY ANYTHING, I HAVE TO GET THIS OFF MY CHEST!

I KNOW IT SOUNDS LIKE THE BEER, SCOTCH, ABSINTHE, AND GRAIN ALCOHOL TALKING, BUT I FELL IN LOVE WITH YOU TODAY!

WILL YOU DO ME THE HONOR OF BEING MY PRINCESS?

YOU WILL?

YOU'VE MADE ME THE HAPPIEST PRINCE IN THE WORLD!

HEY!

NO, HE'S RIGHT. THEY CALL YOU THE HAPPY PRINCE, BUT YOU'RE REALLY A DOWNER!

AND SO...

WE ARE GATHERED HERE TODAY TO JOIN THIS COUPLE IN ROYAL WEDDED BLISS. DO YOU TAKE PRINCE HOMER AS YOUR HUSBAND?

JUST SAY "I DO"!

COME ON, SWEETIE.

I HAVE TO HEAR AN "I DO"!

WELL?

FINE! DOES ANYONE WANT TO BE MY REBOUND BRIDE?

SURE, WHY NOT!

IF YOUR TRUE LOVE MARRIES SOMEONE ELSE, YOU'LL TURN TO FOAM!

WHY SO GLUM, MY LIEGE? MARRIED LIFE NOT TREATING YOU WELL?

IT TURNS OUT WE HAD WHAT SHE CALLED "IRRECONCILABLE DIFFERENCES" AND HAD TO GET...WHAT'S THAT THING CALLED?

AN ANNULMENT?

IF THAT'S THE ONE WITH THE GUILLOTINE, THEN YEAH!

HAVE ANOTHER BEER!

WELL HELLO, HANDSOME!

HUH?

WHAT HAPPENED TO YOU?

IT'S A LONG STORY, BUT I STILL LOVE YOU! I JUST COULDN'T SAY IT BEFORE!

AND SO PRINCE HOMER MARRIED A MUG OF BEER BECAUSE HE WAS ROYALTY, AND THEY COULD DO WHATEVER THEY WANTED BACK THEN.

NOTHING IN THE BIBLE AGAINST IT, EITHER! I NOW PRONOUNCE YOU MAN AND ALE!

# THE PRINCE AND THE PEA

ONCE UPON A TIME THERE WAS A KNOCK AT A PALACE DOOR...

*KNOCK KNOCK!*

WHO COULD IT BE AT THIS HOUR?

OH HELLO, LOWLY SERVANT. I'M A PRINCE WHO WAS AT A COSTUME PARTY WHERE I WAS DRESSED AS A PEASANT. I HAD A FEW TOO MANY HOT MEAD TODDIES, WANDERED OFF, AND GOT LOST IN THE WOODS.

I NEED A PLACE TO STAY THE NIGHT.

WAIT A MINUTE, ASIDE FROM YOUR GOOD LOOKS, WHAT PROOF DO YOU HAVE THAT YOU'RE ROYALTY?

MY MEDICAL BRACELET SAYS I'M A HEMOPHILIAC. ALSO, I'M BARELY TOLERATING TALKING TO SOMEONE AS POOR AS YOURSELF.

ALL RIGHT, I'LL SET UP YOUR BED CHAMBER!

THEN HOP TO IT, MAN!

THERE MUST BE SOME WAY TO DISCOVER IF HE'S REALLY A PRINCE.

HERE YOU GO, YOUR MAJESTY.

I HOPE YOU WILL ENJOY YOUR...

STOP YOUR TOWER OF BABBLING AND TELL ME THE MEANING OF THIS!

AS A MEMBER OF HIGH SOCIETY, I ASSUMED YOU'D WANT TO SLEEP AS FAR AWAY FROM IS COMMON FOLK ON THE GROUND AS POSSIBLE.

RIGHT YOU ARE!

NOW, UNLESS YOU EXPECT ME TO CLIMB THIS LADDER ON MY OWN...!

HERE YOU GO, YOUR MAJESTY. PLEASANT DREAMS!

NOW, IF HE FEELS THE SMALL PEA I PLACED UNDER THE BOTTOM MATTRESS, I'LL KNOW HE'S A TRUE PRINCE OF THE REALM.

KRUSTY BRAND BED PEAS

THE NEXT DAY...

GOOD MORNING, YOUR HIGHNESS! HOW DID YOU SLEEP?

NOT A WINK! SOME SCALAWAG MUST HAVE PEA-ED THE BED!

YOU *ARE* A PRINCE!

WELL, OF COURSE I AM. ⸘YAWN‽!

NOW, I DEMAND BREAKFAST! QUAIL EGGS! DUCK BACON! GOOSE TOAST!

MY COMPLIMENTS! THIS CARPET IS SO SOFT, IT FEELS LIKE I'M WALKING ON AIR!

THUD SNAP CRASH

AND SO...

WHAT ARE *YOU* IN FOR? I THREW A TOMATO AT THE KING.

I STABBED A DUKE WITH A CARROT!

I KILLED A HANDSOME PRINCE WITH A PEA. I GOT LIFE IN PRISON FOR *VEGICIDE REGICIDE!*

AND PARENTS STILL TELL THEIR KIDS VEGETABLES ARE GOOD FOR THEM. WHEN WILL THEY LEARN?

51

:SOB! SOB!:

WHAT'S WRONG?

NO ONE LOVES ME BECAUSE I'M SO UGLY!

LOOKS AREN'T EVERY-THING!

WELL SURE, *YOU'D* SAY THAT. YOU'RE EVEN UGLIER THAN *ME*!

NUH-UH.

MOM, CAN HE LIVE WITH US?

AS LONG AS HE BEHAVES HIMSELF, HAS GOOD MANNERS, AND DOES HIS CHORES!

I GOTTA BE HONEST, LADY. PROBABLY NONE OF THAT'S GONNA HAPPEN.

OH WELL, IT'S NOT LIKE I HAVEN'T COMPROMISED BEFORE!

:BRAAAAP!:

LATER...

WOW! THANKS FOR MAKING ME A PART OF YOUR FAMILY! I'M REALLY HAPPY!

YOU'RE HAPPY BECAUSE YOU FOUND OUT BEAUTY IS JUST SKIN DEEP AND THE IMPORTANT THING IS TO BE YOURSELF?

NO, I'M HAPPY BECAUSE IT'S DUCK SEASON, NOT SWAN SEASON!

YEE-HAW HAW!

BLAM

BAM

DUCK SEASON

ONCE UPON A TIME, THERE WAS A VERY LAZY MAN.

CAN YOU HELP ME REACH THAT BOOK?

THE SNOW QUEEN

THE SNOW QUEEN

## THE SHADOW

I WOULD ADVISE YOU TO FIRST PURCHASE A LADDER FROM THE HARDWARE STORE DOWN THE STREET.

WHEN I REACH UPWARDS, MY SHIRT RISES UP AND MY EXPOSED BELLY BECOMES THE SUBJECT OF TITTERING.

WELL THEN, I'LL JUST BUY MY BOOK *SOMEWHERE ELSE*.

I THINK YOU WILL FIND I AM THE *ONLY* BOOKSELLER IN THIS PATHETIC ONE PRINTING PRESS TOWN. THERE *IS* NO REPLACEMENT FOR ME!

HEY, IT'S SUNSET. HOW COME YOU DON'T HAVE A SHADOW LIKE EVERYTHING ELSE?

WHAT? THAT'S RIDICULOUS! IT'S BARELY WORTH TURNING MY HEAD TO CONFIRM YOUR FOOLISHNESS!

¡GASP!¿ THE LAD SPEAKS *TRUE!*

WELL THE RESULTS FROM YOUR LEECH BLOODLETTING CAME BACK AND AS USUAL IT WAS POINTLESS. AS FOR YOUR PROBLEM, I'VE NEVER SEEN ANYTHING LIKE IT. MOST SHADOWS DON'T HAVE ANY MASS AT ALL.

BUT YOU BEING SO HEAVY, IT MUST HAVE ACTUALLY STARTED TO WEIGH ENOUGH TO BREAK FREE!

YOU MEAN...?

I'M SORRY... YES. YOU'LL NEVER MAKE SHADOW PUPPETS AGAIN.

THIS WILL NOT STAND! I CHALLENGE YOU TO A FIGHT! THE WINNER GETS MY LIFE!

OH, YOU WANT TO SHADOW BOX, DO YOU? FAIR ENOUGH!

WHIFF!

ARE YOU DONE?

¡GASP! ¡WHEEZE!

PLEASE. THIS STORE IS ALL I HAVE. LET ME WORK HERE AT LEAST.

WELL, THERE IS ONE JOB AVAILABLE.

NEW NOVEL COMING SOON: THE RED SHOES

¡MOAN!

OH, PIPE DOWN! SHADOWS DON'T TALK! AND REMEMBER, COME LATE AFTERNOON, I WANT TO SEE YOU GETTING LONGER!

# THUMBELINA

SO, DOC, IS IT A BOY OR A GIRL?

IT'S A HEALTHY, HAPPY LITTLE GIRL!

WHERE?

YOU HAVE TO SQUINT A BIT. IT IS AN ABNORMALLY SMALL BIRTH WEIGHT. DID ANYONE SMOKE AROUND THE MOTHER?

ER...

NOT THAT WE REMEMBER...

AND AFTER A FEW YEARS...

MMMM... THESE ARE GREAT BOAR CHOPS!

MAY I HAVE SOME MORE SALAD?

HOW WAS SCHOOL TODAY?

WHATEVER YOU HEARD, I CAN EXPLAIN!

I GOT ALL A'S ON MY REPORT CARD!

DOES ANYONE ELSE HEAR AN ANNOYING SQUEAKING SOUND?

THAT'S *ME*! HELLO! DOWN HERE!

FINE! IF *THAT'S* THE WAY THINGS ARE, I'LL RUN AWAY UNTIL I FIND A WAY TO GET THEM TO *NOTICE* ME!

I'M SURE I'LL BE FINE. WHAT'S THE WORST THAT COULD HAPPEN?

THWACK!

HEY, IT'S RUDE FOR FOOD TO SIGH WHEN MY MOUTH IS FULL!

≋SIGH!≋

CAN I CONVINCE YOU TO NOT EAT ME?

MAYBE. I'M LOOKING FOR A WIFE FOR MY SON!

MY BREATH SMELLS LIKE FLIES!

OKAY, ON SECOND THOUGHT, I'M GOOD WITH BEING EATEN!

GRAB HOLD OF MY THORAX, IF YOU WANT TO LIVE ≋GA-HEY!≋

59

COME ON! YOU CALL THIS GUY A CHALLENGE? JUST *LOOK* AT HIM!

UM...I CAN *HEAR* YOU!

I'M TRYING TO HELP YOU. PLAY ALONG!

I GUESS YOU'RE RIGHT. BULLYING HIM EVERY DAY IS GETTING' KINDA OLD!

WHAT IF I HAD A *NEW JOB* FOR YOU?

DOES IT INVOLVE SENSELESS VIOLENCE?

AND SO...

GREAT GRILLED GRINCH, HONEY!

WILL YOU PLEASE PASS THE BUTTER?

SLAP!

THE LADY SAID SHE WANTS THE BUTTER!

YESSIR, MR. SPRITE, SIR!

EXCELLENT!

# THE GOOD MOTHER

MY HAIR?

BLARG!

HAND ME THE SCISSORS!

SHORTLY...

MY CHILDREN ARE WORTH ANY PRICE.

THANKS FOR THE ADDRESS!

PURRRRR!

HE LIVES AT THE CORNER OF ELYSIAN AND TARTARUS. THAT'S DOESN'T SOUND TOO FAR AWAY.

PHONE BOOK OF THE DEAD

TWO YEARS LATER...

ALL RIGHT, THAT WAS FARTHER THAN IT SEEMED.

NOW WHAT? A RIVER? BUT I CAN'T SWIM!

⁑SOB!⁑ BUT I'M SO CLOSE! OH, KIDS, I'M SO SORRY! I'VE FAILED YOU!

PLINK!

PLUNK!

DID YOU JUST CRY YOUR EYES OUT?

I SUPPOSE SO. WHO'S TALKING TO ME?

EEEEEEW! THAT IS SOOOOO GROSS!

HERE, TAKE THEM BACK!

PTTUUUU!!

BUT MY CHILDREN ARE STILL TRAPPED ON THE OTHER SIDE OF YOU!

JUST GO, AND DON'T DROP ANY MORE OF YOUR ORGANS IN ME!

THIS MUST BE IT!

DEATH'S DOOR
NO SALESMEN

DEATH! AT LAST!

CAN THIS WAIT? I'M PACKING!

DEATH'S TAKING A HOLIDAY!

DEATH'S DOOR
NO SALESMEN

SO YOU SEE, HANS CHRISTIAN ANDERSEN IS NOTHING TO BE AFRAID OF!

ROD? TODD?!

OH SORRY, LISA. ROD GOT SCARED WHEN THE MAN FELL OUT OF THE BOAT, AND WE'VE BEEN READING OUR OWN BOOK SINCE THEN.

WHAT ARE YOU READING?

VEGEMITE TALES! THEY'RE MORAL STORIES TOLD USING AUSTRALIAN FOOD PRODUCTS!

WANNA READ WITH US?

WHY NOT?

LISTEN, SHRIMPY, YOU'D BETTER BE TELLING BRUCE YOU STOLE HIS BOOMERANG, OR WHEN YOU DIE, YOU'LL END UP IN THE OTHER LAND DOWN UNDER.

AND THAT'S ONE BARBIE, I DON'T WANT TO END UP ON! I'VE LEARNED MY LESSON, MATE!

⋮SIGH!⋮

THE END

# ARABIAN

# TALES

ARE YOU SURE YOU WANT TO GO OUT? YOU LOOK *TIRED*.

≷YAWN!≷ YEAH, I JUST CAN'T GET TO SLEEP AT NIGHT!

MAYBE HAVING MY BEDROOM RIGHT NEXT TO THE TORTURE CHAMBER WASN'T THE GREATEST IDEA. MAN, THOSE GUYS NEVER SHUT UP!

WHY DON'T I TELL YOU SOME STORIES TO HELP YOU SLEEP?

WHY NOT? AND IF I LIKE THEM, YOU CAN LIVE ANOTHER NIGHT!

SOUNDS GOOD TO ME!

ONCE UPON A TIME THERE WAS A POOR MAN WHO FOUND A MAGICAL LAMP!

THE NAME'S *ALADDIN!* SO ARE YOU A *REAL* GENIE? DO I GET *THREE* WISHES?

WHOA WHOA WHOA, SLOW DOWN!

YEAH, YOU'VE GOT THREE WISHES. BUT WHY IS EVERYTHING ABOUT *YOU?*

LOOK AT ME! I HAVEN'T HAD A THING TO DRINK IN A THOUSAND YEARS!

THEN YOU SHOULD HAVE A DRINK!

WISH NUMBER ONE HAS BEEN GRANTED!

POOF!

HEY!

GENIE RULE NUMBER ONE! NO TAKE BACKS!

OKAY, THIS TIME I WISH MY FAMILY HAD ENOUGH TO EAT!

OKAY, CHECK THIS OUT! A LITTLE ABRACA-DAB'LL DO YA!

BLESS IS TEN

ALADDIN'S ALL-YOU-CAN-EAT BUFFET AND 'GO-GO' BAR

BUFFET

:GASP!: AVERT YOUR EYES, BOYS!

DADDY?

WHY ARE THOSE LADIES IN CAGES IN THEIR UNDERWEAR?

WISH NUMBER TWO IS GRANTED! SO WHAT DO YOU THINK?

AW NO! THIS IS JUST GOING TO BE ONE OF YOUR TRICKS, YOU MEANIE GENIE!

I SAY I WANT HER BACK TO THE WAY SHE USED TO BE, AND YOU'LL JUST CHANGE HER INTO A BABY OR SOMETHING! AM I RIGHT?

HEH HEH! THAT WOULD BE A GOOD ONE!

I WISH YOU'D ESCORT YOURSELF OUT OF TOWN!

WISH GRANTED! YOU HEARD THE MAN! GET LOST!

HEY! WATCH IT! I BRUISE MYSELF EASILY!

POOF!

CAN I AT LEAST HAVE A DRINK BEFORE I GET KICKED OUT?

WELL, THAT DOES SOUND FAIR!

AND SO, SHORTLY...

ARE YOU REALLY OUR MOMMY?

SHE'D BE NEAT TO HAVE AROUND ON HALLOWEEN...*IF* WE CELEBRATED IT!

WAIT UNTIL MY MOTHER HEARS WHAT YOU WERE UP TO WHILE I WAS GONE!

YOU KNOW WHO'S A GREAT GUY? *YOU!*

NO, NO! SHUT UP! *YOU'RE* THE BEST!

YOUR MOTHER? BUT SHE'S *DEAD!*

AND I EXPECT YOU TO BRING HER BACK AS WELL!

YO, AL! YOUR OLD LADY SAID IT'D BE COOL IF WE CRASHED AT YOUR PLACE UNTIL WE'RE BACK ON OUR FEET!

YEAH, BUT GET THIS! WE DON'T *HAVE* FEET!

¡GRRRR!¿

OW!

OH, SURE'N YOU FOUND ME POT O' GOLD. NOW I HAVE TO GRANT YOUR GREATEST WISH!

CLANG!

BOOT!

MAN, CARRYING ALL THIS STUFF WAS EASIER WHEN WE HAD *FORTY* THIEVES.

WELL, THE OTHER THIRTY-SIX WANTED MEDICAL AND DENTAL, SO WE HAD TO LET THEM GO!

DISCOUNT OLIVES

WHY, THOSE DIRTY THIEVING THIEVES! SO *THEY* ARE THE ONES WHO HAVE BEEN ROBBING MY STORE!

WANNA CHECK IF WE'RE BEING FOLLOWED?

NAH, I SLEPT ON A ROCK LAST NIGHT AND GOT A STIFF NECK. I'M GONNA STICK WITH LOOKING STRAIGHT AHEAD!

OPEN SESAME!

THE *ROCK!* IT IS *ROLLING!* OH, IF ONLY WE HAD SUCH A SECURITY SYSTEM AT THE STORE ...OR AT LEAST A FOURTH WALL.

LATER...

FINALLY! THEY ARE LEAVING! NOW IS MY CHANCE!

OPEN...UM... *SESAME?*

⧉GASP!⧉ IT IS A YEAR'S WORTH OF SHOPLIFTED MERCHANDISE!

CAMEL JERKY

CAMEL CHOW

DISCOUNT OLIVES

WELL, IT IS TIME TO GET YOU BACK ON MY SHELVES WHERE I CAN OVER-PRICE YOU!

WHAM!

CAM CHOW

DISCOUN OLIVE

WHO ARE *YOU?*

*SESAME!* YOU DON'T THINK THAT ROCK MOVES *ITSELF* DO YOU?

MANY, MANY TRIPS LATER...

OUR STUFF! SOMEONE SWIPED IT!

THIS IS GOING TO LOOK REALLY BAD AT OUR NEXT SHAREHOLDERS MEETING!

I RECOGNIZE THOSE SANDAL PRINTS! IT'S APU BABA THE SHOPKEEPER!

YOU RECOGNIZE SANDAL PRINTS?

I ADMIRE A GOOD PAIR OF SHOES! SO WHAT?

DUMMY UP, YOU TWO! I HAVE A PLAN!

HELLO, STRANGER! HOW MAY I SERVE YOU TODAY IN MY FULLY-STOCKED SHOP?

PERSIAN NIC BLANKETS

CAMEL CHOW

CAMEL JERKY

CAMEL JERKY

KY

$ $ $ $

HELLO! I'M FROM THE SHEIK-E-MART HEAD OFFICE IN...WHEREVER THAT IS. I'VE GOT A NEW COLD DRINK DISPENSER THAT MAKES SOMETHING CALLED A SQUISHEE!

SQUISHEE MACHINE

I'LL SET IT UP FOR YOU. JUST FORGET IT'S EVEN HERE!

VERY WELL, IF YOU NEED ME I SHALL BE CHANGING THE EXPIRATION DATE ON THE CHICKPEAS!

HE'S FALLEN FOR IT. NOW ALL WE HAVE TO DO IS WAIT UNTIL HE GETS TIRED, AND WHEN HE LEAST EXPECTS IT, WE ALL JUMP HIM, BEAT HIM WITHIN AN INCH OF HIS LIFE, AND TAKE EVERY-THING BACK!

OH, MR. INSTALLER MAN, I...

NOW WHERE DID HE GO?

OH WELL, SINCE I HAVE NOTHING TO FEAR, I'LL JUST TURN MY BACK TO THE MACHINE AND TAKE A NAP.

AWESOME PLAN!

OKAY, I DON'T KNOW WHOSE HAND THAT IS ON MY BUTT, BUT IT BETTER BE THAT MINE'S JUST FALLEN ASLEEP!

ANY SECOND NOW!

BUT BEFORE I DO, I SHOULD FILL THE SQUISHEE MACHINE. OH NO! I DON'T HAVE ANY COLD WATER FOR THE COLD DRINKS!

I'M SURE THIS SCALDING HOT WATER WILL DO JUST FINE!

SSSSSSS!

81

Y'KNOW, THAT WAS A REALLY GOOD PUSH!

WELL, THEY'RE GOING TO BE GOING FOR A WHILE SO LET'S JUST SWITCH TO THE STORY OF...

# SINBART THE SAILOR

AW, COME ON, GRAMPA! CAN'T I HAVE A LITTLE MORE ALLOWANCE? I BLEW IT ALL ON GETTING MY EAR PIERCED.

YOU SHOULD DO WHAT *I* DID WHEN *I* WAS YOUR AGE!

RIDE A DINOSAUR? INVENT FIRE? BORROW MONEY FROM ADAM AND EVE?

*NO!* I BECAME A *SAILOR!* STILL HAVE MY BOAT! IT'S YOURS IF YOU WANT IT!

THE SEA'S WHERE YOU'LL FIND YOUR FORTUNE!

SOON...

YOU GUYS SEE ANY CASH FLOATING IN THE OCEAN?

NOPE!

NOT YET, OH CAPTAIN, MY CAPTAIN!

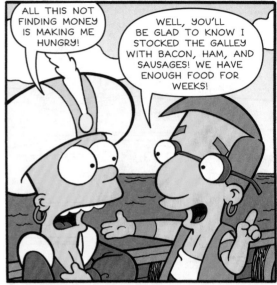

ALL THIS NOT FINDING MONEY IS MAKING ME HUNGRY!

WELL, YOU'LL BE GLAD TO KNOW I STOCKED THE GALLEY WITH BACON, HAM, AND SAUSAGES! WE HAVE ENOUGH FOOD FOR WEEKS!

MAYBE I SHOULDN'T HAVE TOLD THE DOG TO GUARD IT!

¡WHIMPER!

SAUSAGE

BACON

BACON

SAUSAGE

HAM

NONE OF THESE TREES POSSESS FRUIT. HOW ODD.

DOES ANYONE ELSE SMELL FISH?

I SMELL IT, BUT NONE ARE BITING!

OH, ALLAH, I KNOW I DON'T PRAY TO YOU MUCH, EXCEPT AT THE HOLIDAYS, BUT PLEASE LET US GET JUST ONE BITE.

ONE VOYAGE LATER...

SO, SINBART, DOES THIS ISLAND HAVE RICHES?

WELL, THERE'S GOOD NEWS, BAD NEWS, GOOD NEWS, BAD NEWS, AND GOOD NEWS.

WHAT'S THE GOOD NEWS?

THE ISLAND IS COVERED IN GIANT DIAMONDS.

WHAT'S THE BAD NEWS?

IT'S GUARDED BY GIANT SNAKES!

AND THE GOOD NEWS?

SSSS!

CAW!

THERE ARE GIANT SNAKE-EATING BIRDS!

AND THE BAD NEWS?

THE BIRDS EAT PEOPLE, TOO!

AND THE GOOD NEWS?

THEY FILLED UP ON MARTIN!

LET'S GO!

YET ANOTHER VOYAGE LATER...

CLINK

CLINK

H-HEY, SINBART, WHY ARE WE FIGHTING THESE SKELETONS AGAIN?

BECAUSE IT SURE LOOKS COOL!

OOPS! SORRY, LADY!

OH DEAR!

MAUDE!

AND ANOTHER VOY-- OH, YOU GET THE IDEA...

THERE'S NO TIME FOR LOVE, SINBART! WE HAVE TREASURE HUNTING TO DO!

I WANT YOU TO MEET MY FATHER, THE KING OF THE ISLAND!

HELLO, YOUNG MAN. WOULD YOU LIKE SOME SUNFLOWER SEEDS?

SURE!

OH, DAD!

WHAT? ⸨MUNCH!⸩

NOW THAT YOU ACCEPTED MY FATHER'S GIFT OF SEEDS, WE'RE MARRIED! IT'S THE LAW OF THE ISLAND!

AW, MAN!

IS IT JUST ME OR DOES THAT ROCK LOOK LIKE IT'S GETTING BIGGER?

THE END

# "ANTONY and CLEOPATRA"

I CAN'T BELIEVE HE'S *LATE*. THIS COUNSELING WAS *HIS* IDEA!

FRIENDS, ROMANS, COUNTRYMEN, LEND ME YOUR EARS! I APOLOGIZE FOR MY *TARDINESS!*

YOU SEE, THIS IS WHAT I MEAN! HE HAS *NO RESPECT* FOR MY *NEEDS*.

I COULDN'T JUST LET ROME *FALL*, COULD I?

THE PLACE WAS A MESS. THE STREETS WERE COVERED IN *LITTER*, LEAVES IN THE *AQUADUCTS*, AND DON'T GET ME STARTED ON THE *VOMITORIUMS!*

ALWAYS WITH THE VOMITORIUMS! I KNEW THIS WAS A WASTE OF TIME. YOU'RE THE ONE WITH "*ISSUES*," NOT ME!

YOU SEE? THIS IS WHY THEY CALL HER "QUEEN OF DENIAL!"

IT'S "QUEEN OF *THE NILE*," AND DON'T TELL ME I HAVEN'T TRIED MY BEST IN THIS RELATIONSHIP. HE DOES NOTHING BUT *COMPLAIN*.

MY *SACRED CATS* MAKE HIM *SNEEZE*, MY *PYRAMIDS* ARE *TOO POINTY,* AND NOW HE'S EVEN COMPLAINING ABOUT MY *MILK BATHS!*

I'M *LACTOSE INTOLERANT!* I KISSED HER NECK AND WAS *BLOATED* FOR A WEEK!

SOMETIMES I THINK SHE TOOK CAESAR UP ON HIS REQUEST FOR HER TO *KILL* ME!

OH, SWEET RA, WILL YOU EVER LET THAT GO? I'LL TELL YOU HIS PROBLEM. A *FEAR OF COMMITMENT*.

NOT WANTING TO BE *BURIED ALIVE* WITH YOU WHEN YOU DIE ISN'T A FEAR OF COMMITMENT!

AND TO TOP IT ALL OFF, HE *FORGOT* OUR *ANNIVERSARY*.

DID I?

OH, ANTONY! YOU REMEMBERED!

AN *ASP!* OH, YOU SHOULDN'T HAVE.

THESE ARE SO EXPENSIVE TO GET *POISON-FREE*.

EXCUSE ME?

GAAAAH!

*LUNGE!*

SO, UM...ASIDE FROM THE *FATAL VENOM*, HOW DO YOU LIKE THE GIFT?

IT'S LIKE EVERYTHING ELSE IN THIS RELATIONSHIP, ANTONY...

...IT *BITES!*

# "JULIUS CAESAR"

HAPPY FEAST OF LUPERCAL, MR. CAESAR.

AH, THE PEOPLE *LOVE ME*. DO THEY NOT, BRUTUS?

WE ALL DO, SIR.

!

SWISH!

THUNK!

OH, A *COIN* WITH MY FACE ON IT! THAT'S *GOOD LUCK!*

"RENDER UNTO CAESAR WHAT IS CAESAR'S," I ALWAYS SAY. YOU KNOW, WE SHOULD BUILD A *FACTORY* THAT JUST RENDERS THINGS TO ME. WE COULD CALL IT A *RENDERING PLANT*.

EXCELLENT IDEA, SIR. BUT FOR NOW, *THE SENATE* IS WAITING FOR US.

AHOY-HOY, SENATE!

HAIL, CAESAR!

OH, MARK ANTONY, HOW ARE THINGS WITH THAT *SAUCY EGYPTIAN* YOU'VE BEEN COURTING?

DON'T ASK.

BEFORE WE GET TO BUSINESS, I WANT TO HOLD A *PICNIC* IN HONOR OF MYSELF TOMORROW. WHAT WILL THE *WEATHER* BE LIKE?

HAIL, CAESAR.

YES, HAIL YOURSELF. BUT WHAT'S THE *WEATHER* GOING TO BE LIKE?

HAIL, CAESAR.

OKAY, HELLO TO YOU TOO! ALL I WANT TO KNOW IS... *THE WEATHER!*

HAIL... CAESAR!

OKAY, FORGET THE WEATHER! LET'S TALK ABOUT *THE MEAL*.

I WANT THAT *DELICIOUS SALAD* YOU MADE THE LAST TIME WITH THE *ROMAINE LETTUCE*. WHAT WAS IT CALLED AGAIN?

CAESAR.

YES, WHAT WAS IT *CALLED?*

CAESAR.

HAVE HIM *FLOGGED!*

SIR, THAT'S *VERY PAINFUL*. HAVE MERCY.

OH, DEAR!

VERY WELL, KILL HIM *FIRST*.

MAN, THAT GUY'S *NUTS!*

YOU SAID IT, *CALIGULA!*

I WAS TALKING TO THE *OTHER* SENATOR.

?

NOW, IF THERE IS NO FURTHER BUSINESS...

*SWISH!*

...AH, ANOTHER COIN!

*ROAR!*

MAN, I WASTED MY LAST LION!

DOES THAT MEAN WE *CHRISTIANS* CAN GO? OR DO YOU HAVE ANY OTHER ANIMALS YOU'D LIKE TO *FEED US* TO?

WELL, I'M OFF TO THE BATHS. WILL I SEE YOU THERE, BRUTUS?

YOU KNOW YOU WILL, SIR!

I'M HAVING **SECOND THOUGHTS** ABOUT THE **ASSASSINATION**.

NO WAY, BLUTO.

BRUTUS.

WHATEVER, THERE'S NO BACKING OUT NOW! TONIGHT, WE **KILL** JULIUS CAESAR **AND** MARK ANTONY!

HEY!

OOPS! NO, NOT YOU! I MEAN MARK... UM...MARK...

...MARK HAMILL!

A SHORT WHILE LATER...

OKAY, BACK TO ROME!

MAYBE WE CAN JUST LET HIM OFF WITH A **STERN WARNING** IN THE **SUGGESTION BOX**.

THE SENATE! WHAT, IS THIS SOME SORT OF PARTY IN MY HONOR?

UM...KIND OF ...A **SURPRISE PARTY**.

SURPRISE!

STAB!

OOPS.

:SIGH.: LET'S DO THIS QUICKLY.

WHAT'S WITH ALL THIS *LYING AROUND* HOLDING YOUR STOMACHS? WHERE ARE THE *BALLOONS*? WHERE'S THE *CAKE*?

HE WAS *TOO THIN*. WE ALL *MISSED HIM* AND *STABBED EACH OTHER*. THANK, JUPITER!

HERE YOU GO.

WHAT? WHERE DID YOU GET A *CAKE*?

I ALWAYS CARRY ONE WITH ME...JUST IN CASE.

HOLD THE CHARIOT! TWO PIECES ARE *MISSING*.

I ATE ONE PIECE, BUT *PLANNING ASSASSINATIONS* MAKES ME *HUNGRY*, SO I...

DON'T SAY IT.

...ATE TWO, BRUTUS.

:GROAN!:

OH, ROMEO, SWEAR NOT BY THE MOON.

SWEAR NOT BY THE FENCE.

JUST STOP *SWEARING* ALREADY! YOU'LL WAKE UP *MY* PARENTS!

I STUBBED MY TOE ON YOUR @#!! GARDEN GNOME!

"Romeo and Juliet"

LISTEN AND HEAR THE *SAD STORY* OF *TWO STAR-CROSSED LOVERS*.

WHATEVER THAT MEANS.

HOP!

HOP!

HOP!

VERONA IS A NICE PLACE FOR PEOPLE TO LIVE AND STUFF...

HELLO, YOUNG MAN!

GOODDAY TO YOU, FAIR NARRATOR!

...EXCEPT FOR THE *FAMILY FEUD*.

"IN THIS CORNER WE HAVE THE CAPULET FAMILY, READY FOR ACTION."

I'LL TEACH YOU TO *BITE YOUR THUMB* AT ME!

I WAS JUST BITING MY THUMB.

"AND THE MONTAGUES. UM... WHERE ARE YOUR FAMILY?"

IN *JAIL*. THE *BAIL BONDSMAN* WOULDN'T RETURN THEIR CALL AFTER DAD BOUNCED THAT LAST CHECK TO HIM.

JUST GET ON WITH THE STORY, OR I'LL POUND YA!

SO THEIR *FORBIDDEN LOVE* WAS A *SECRET*. LIKE THE LOVE BETWEEN MY OCTOPUS, MR. INKS, AND MY GIRAFFE, SPOT.

OH, ROMEO, DOST THOU *LOVE* ME?

Y'KNOW, WHATEVER.

CAN I COME UP THERE AND *KISS* YA?

IT IS ALL I WISH FAIR ROMEO, BUT MY *NURSE* MIGHT HEAR AND TELL MY PARENTS!

YEAH, LIKE I CARE. I HAVE TO CHANGE YOUR FATHER'S *BED-PAN*.

HE'S SICK?

NO, JUST REALLY *LAZY*.

I HAVE TO GET READY FOR MY *WEDDING* TONIGHT. I'M GOING TO TRY AND GET OUT OF THAT, AND I'LL KISS YOU AFTER. SEE YOU LATER?

YEAH, OKAY I GUESS.

DUDE, WHAT'S HAPPENED TO YOU?

YOU WERE LISTENING?

YEAH, AND YOU'RE MORE *WHIPPED* THAN MERINGUE PIE.

AT LEAST MY GIRLFRIEND IS *REAL*.

KELLY'S REAL. SHE JUST LIVES IN... UM...CANADA.

LAST TIME YOU SAID IT WAS *ICELAND*.

THAT'S *IT! LET'S DUEL!*

*CHILL*, TYBALT. YOUR PAROLE OFFICER SAID NO MORE DEATH DUELS AND...*OW!*

HEY, MERCUTIO, GET OUT OF MY *SWORD'S WAY!*

STAB!

SHORTLY...

OW! I SHOWED YOU WHERE HER *TOMB* IS. WHAT ARE YOU HITTING ME FOR?

I'M WORKING THROUGH SOME *GRIEF*.

AW, MAN, IT'S *TRUE!* SHE'S *DEAD*.

OH, MY LOVE. ALL THE THINGS I NEVER GOT A CHANCE TO SAY. WELL, NOW I WILL!

I THINK WE SHOULD SEE *OTHER PEOPLE*.

IT'S NOT YOU, IT'S *ME*. WELL YOU BEING *DEAD* AND EVERYTHING... I GUESS IT IS *YOU*. I HOPE WE CAN STILL BE *FRIENDS*.

IT'D BE COOL HAVING A *CORPSE* FOR A PAL.

YOU *JERK!* I'M DEAD, AND YOU *BREAK UP WITH ME!*

AHHHH! A *ZOMBIE!*

I WAS JUST *FAKING* BEING DEAD TO BE WITH YOU.

I DIDN'T KNOW THAT! WHAT DID YOU EXPECT ME TO DO?

*DRINK POISON*, THEN *I'D* THINK *YOU* WERE *DEAD*, AND *STAB MYSELF IN THE HEART!*

IT'D BE THE *MOST ROMANTIC STORY EVER*.

I COULD STAB YOU WITH MY SWORD IF YOU'D LIKE.

ARRRGH! YOU ARE *SO FRUSTRATING!*

YOU KNOW, I DON'T THINK I'LL EVER UNDERSTAND GIRLS.

I HEAR YA. WANNA PLAY HIDE AND SEEK?

YOU'RE ON!

GOOD AFTERNOON!

MA'AM!

TOP OF THE DAY TO YOU.

PLEASANT WEATHER WE'RE HAVING.

HOW DO YOU DO?

GREETINGS, M'LADY!

Y'KNOW, THIS "BEING A GENTLEMAN STUFF" IS... WHATAYACALL IT? NOT WORKING.

WANNA GO TO MOES? IT'S *LADIES NIGHT*.

YOU MERRY WIVES OF WINDSOR REALLY AIN'T ALL THAT MERRY.

THE *MERRY* KICKS IN AFTER A FEW *MORE DRINKS*.

KEEP 'EM COMING, BOYS!

# RICHARD III

NOW IS THE WINTER OF OUR *DISCONTENT*.

I MEAN HAVE YOU SEEN *OUR NUMBERS*? WE'RE BEING *SLAUGHTERED* BY ALL THE *CHRISTMAS SPECIALS*!

HERE'S TEN GRAND. BREAK RUDOLPH'S KNEECAPS!

BUT YOUR MAJESTY, HE IS A *PUPPET*.

THEN CLIP HIS STRINGS. GEEZ, DO THEY EVEN TRAIN YOU GOONS ANYMORE? NOW SCRAM, I'M ON IN ONE MINUTE.

:SIGH.: WAS IT ALL WORTHWHILE? SURE, I'M *THE KING OF COMEDY*, BUT ALL THOSE I'VE CRUSHED ON MY WAY TO THE TOP...

...WAS IT ALL WORTH IT FOR THE *MONEY*, *FAME*, AND *POWER*?

HEH, HEH! MAN I ALWAYS MAKE MYSELF LAUGH WITH THAT JOKE!

HEY, HEY! IT'S GREAT TO BE DOING THE SHOW HERE IN *BOSWORTH*! WHO *DO YOU LOVE*?!

LET'S START WITH AN *"ITCHY AND SCRATCHY CARTOON"*!

KING RICHARD!

AW, MAN, I'M LOSING THEM.

TIME TO DO *THE COWBOY SKETCH*.

BOOOOO!

HOWDY, Y'ALL! THE BANK'S BEEN ROBBED, AND I THINK THAT DURN HOMBRE *OTHELLO* DID IT. WHY DO I THINK THAT?

I'VE GOT A *HUNCH!*

OOOOKAY, RIGHT TO *THE STUNT RIDING*.

KRUSTY I WOULDN'T DO THAT.

SPROING!

GAH!

WHOA!

WHY DID HE KILL THAT HORSE, MOMMY?

AAAAH!

WHAM!

A HORSE! A HORSE! MY KINGDOM FOR TWO *NON-UNION ACTORS* TO PLAY A HORSE.

RICHARD, I'M HERE TO KILL YOU.

AND BY YOU, I MEAN YOUR SHOW. I'M THE *NEW HEAD OF PROGRAMMING* AND YOUR SHOW IS BEING PUT ON *HIATUS* INDEFINITELY FOR *RETOOLING*.

SIDESHOW RICHMOND? BUT I CRUSHED YOU ON MY WAY TO THE TOP.

THEN CONSIDER THIS YOUR *DAILY IRONY SUPPLIMENT*.

YOU'LL NEVER FIND A *REPLACEMENT* FOR ME.

WE ALREADY HAVE. IT'S A NEW SHOW CALLED "KING LEAR."

WHEN'S THAT START?

RIGHT NOW.

"KING LEAR"

HOW ABOUT **YOU**, REGAN?

SO GLAD YOU ASKED, FATHER!

CLAP! CLAP!

HOW MUCH DO I LOVE THEE? **MORE THAN** ALL THE **STARS IN HEAVEN. MORE THAN** ALL THE **GRAINS OF SAND ON THE BEACH. MORE THAN** ALL THE **BEADS OF SWEAT ON A SUBSTITUTE TEACHER'S FORE-HEAD.** WORDS CANNOT EXPRESS MY LOVE, AND SO I SHALL END THIS SENTENCE...NOW.

THE **MONKEYS** WERE A **NICE TOUCH.**

YOUR PRAISE **HUMBLES** ME!

HOW ABOUT **YOU**, CORDELIA?

I LOVE YOU, FATHER.

BUT HOW MUCH?

I LOVE YOU AS A DAUGHTER LOVES A FATHER. I LOVE YOU AS MUCH AS YOU LOVE ME.

THAT'S **ALL**? I'VE NEVER BEEN **SO INSULTED!**

GO TO THE ROOM!

MY ROOM?

NO! *THE BANISHMENT ROOM!*

I DIDN'T EVEN KNOW WE HAD A BANISHMENT ROOM.

BANISHMENT ROOM

AAAAAAAH!

GOOD DECISION, FATHER!

THIS JUST IN, KING LEAR HAS BANISHED HIS DAUGHTER CORDELIA.

IN THIS REPORTER'S OPINION...A *BAD MOVE*, AS SHE WAS HIS *ONLY TRULY LOVING CHILD*. THIS IS LORD KENT REPORTING.

YOU ARE SO BANISHED!

YOU CAN'T BANISH ME! I'M GOING TO *EMIGRATE!*

I HAVE *NO IDEA* WHAT THAT MEANS.

TOSS!

AAAAAAH!

DON'T WORRY, FATHER. WE'LL TAKE CARE OF YOU THE WAY YOU *DESERVE* TO BE TREATED.

THANK YOU, MY CHILDREN.

ONE WEEK LATER...

I FEEL *AWFUL*, LIKE I'VE AGED *FORTY YEARS*. WHAT HAVE YOU BEEN *FEEDING* ME?

WAAAAH!

IT'S NOT *POISON*, SO THAT YOU'LL BE GONE SOON, AND I'LL TAKE OVER, IF THAT'S WHAT YOU'RE THINKING. NOW SHUT UP AND CHANGE GON'S DIAPERS!

WHAT HAVE I DONE?

YOU WERE RIGHT, KENT. I AM SO SORRY FOR NOT LISTENING TO YOU TOO, GENTLE FOOL.

WHAT ARE YOU TALKING ABOUT? WHEN WAS I IN THIS STORY?

WE HAD TO *CUT YOUR SCENE*. IT WASN'T *PLAYING WELL* WITH THE 19-35 *DEMOGRAPHIC*.

I MUST *FIND* MY DAUGHTER. MY SWEET LOVING CHILD!

SOME DOGS WERE CHEWING ON SOMETHING IN THE BUSHES.

OH BY THE GODS, NO!

BLOW, WINDS, AND CRACK YOUR CHEEKS. RAGE, BLOW--

HOLD IT!

WHAT?

SHE'S *TOTALLY FAKING* TO GET *ATTENTION!* SHE DID *THE SAME THING* TO ME!

AAAAH!

ROMEO! YOU SHOULDN'T EVEN BE HERE!

TOLD YA!

YOU ARE SO RUDE...SO RUDE...SO RUDE...

BIBLE STORIES

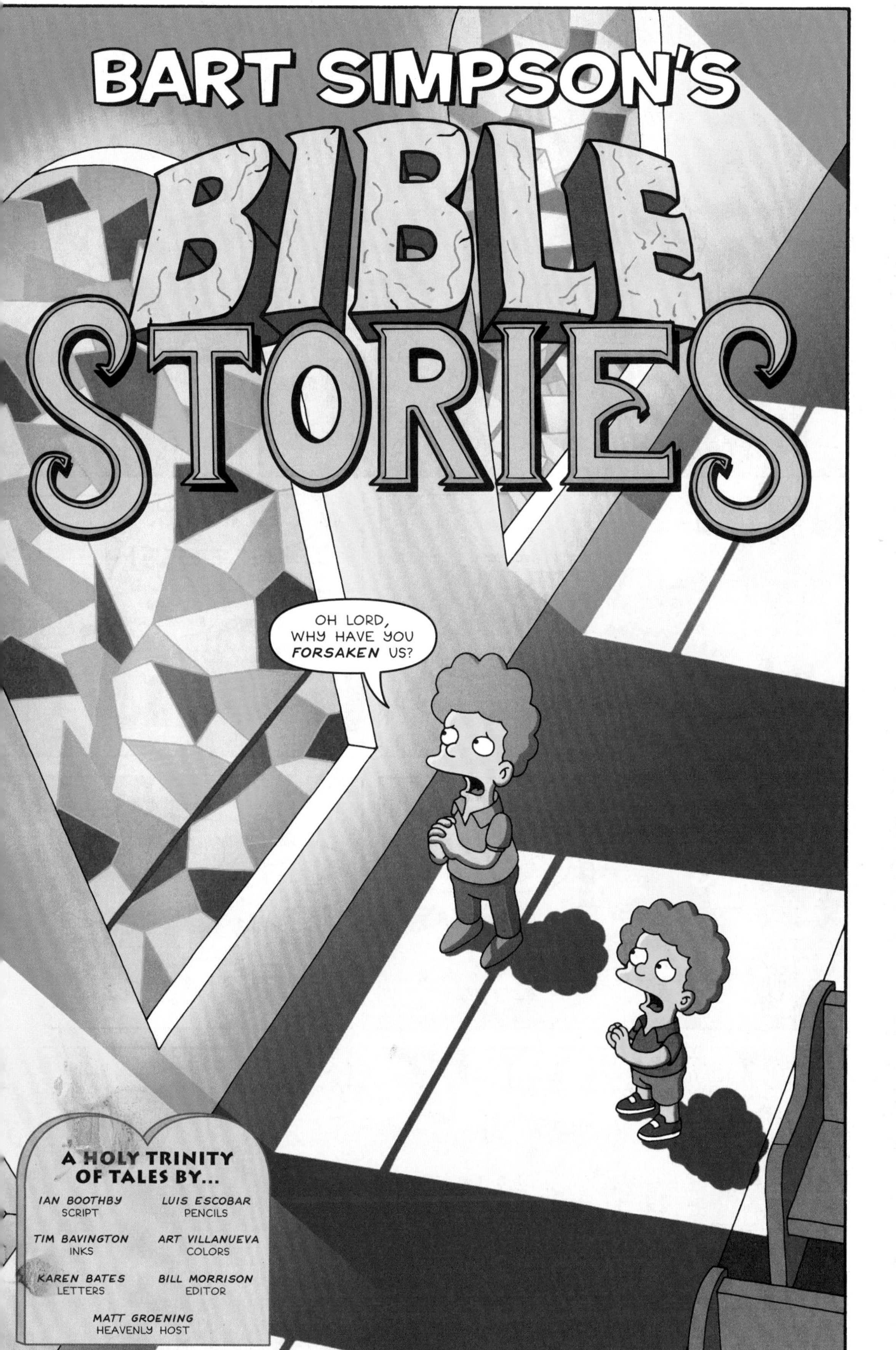

BART SIMPSON'S
BIBLE STORIES
OH LORD, WHY HAVE YOU FORSAKEN US?
A HOLY TRINITY OF TALES BY...
IAN BOOTHBY SCRIPT
LUIS ESCOBAR PENCILS
TIM BAVINGTON INKS
ART VILLANUEVA COLORS
KAREN BATES LETTERS
BILL MORRISON EDITOR
MATT GROENING HEAVENLY HOST

HEY, WHAT'S WITH ALL THE *YELLING*? DID TODD SEE A *CATERPILLAR*?

WORSE!

SUNDAY SCHOOL TEACHER CALLED IN *SICK* TODAY, SO IT WAS CANCELLED.

WHAT'LL WE DO BART? *WHAT'LL WE DO*?!!

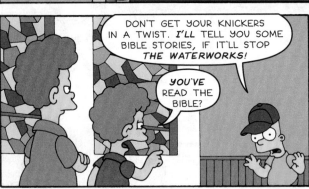

DON'T GET YOUR KNICKERS IN A TWIST. *I'LL* TELL YOU SOME BIBLE STORIES, IF IT'LL STOP *THE WATERWORKS!*

*YOU'VE* READ THE BIBLE?

WELL, I'VE PICKED UP A *FEW STORIES* FROM *TELEVISION*.

BUT DADDY SAYS *CABLE TV* IS *EVIL*.

AND *EXPENSIVE*.

LOOK, GOD MADE *EVERYTHING*, RIGHT?

YES.

AND SO HE MADE TV. AND GOD IS *PERFECT*, RIGHT?

YES.

SO *TV* MUST BE *PERFECT*. RIGHT?

OKAY, BART! TELL US A STORY.

I GUESS SO.

PULL UP A PEW, AND I'LL TELL YOU A TALE OF A FAMILY NOT *TOO DIFFERENT* FROM YOURS OR MINE.

WELL, NOT TOO DIFFERENT FROM *MINE*.

YOU *COULD* HELP WITH THE PLOW SOMETIME!

THAT WOULD BE THE SIN OF *COVETING MY WIFE* WHO HAS THE JOB OF MY OX AND MY ASS.

*I'D* LIKE TO READ THOSE *COMMANDMENTS* YOU'RE ALWAYS QUOTING SOMETIME.

WELL, WELL! LOOK WHO'S BACK!

DAD, I... I SPENT ALL MY MONEY *FOOLISHLY* AND *SELFISHLY.* I'M REALLY SORRY.

WIFE! KILL THE *FATTED CALF* FOR A *FEAST* IN OUR SON'S *HONOR!*

WHAT?!!! WHILE HE'S BEEN OUT HAVING A *GOOD TIME,* I'VE BEEN *SLAVING* ON THIS FARM!

DAUGHTER, WE LOVE YOU, BUT THERE'S MORE *JOY IN HEAVEN* FOR ONE *LOST SHEEP* THAT COMES BACK TO THE FOLD THAN FOR ALL THAT STAY.

BUT HE DOES THIS WITH HIS ALLOWANCE *EVERY WEEK!*

YOU REALLY JUST DO THIS AS AN EXCUSE FOR *FATTED CALF,* DON'T YOU?

CAN'T TALK... HONORING SON BY EATING!

GOD BLESS US, EVERYONE!

YEA, VERILY!

# "ABRAHAM'S SACRIFICE"

ABRAHAM WAS *NINETY-NINE* WHEN GOD SPOKE TO HIM.

ABE, I have a JOB for you!

WHAT'S THAT? SPEAK UP!

I have something I need you to do!

LATER...

HEY THERE, JOB. WHAT'S NEW?

OH HI, ABE. GOD'S BEEN *TESTING* ME.

MY OXEN *DIED*, MY SHEEP WERE *SET ON FIRE*, MY KIDS HAD A HOUSE *FALL* ON 'EM, AND I'M COVERED IN THESE *PAINFUL SORES*.

CAN'T *COMPLAIN* THOUGH. HOW ABOUT YOU?

GOD JUST TOLD ME TO HAVE A BUNCH OF CHILDREN WITH MY BEAUTIFUL WIFE SARAH.

GOD'S *PET*.

UH, MR. JOB? I'VE GOT SOME *BAD NEWS* ABOUT YOUR SERVANTS.

YEARS PASSED AND GOD SPOKE TO ABRAHAM AGAIN...

ABE! You must offer your son as a BURNT SACRIFICE to prove your FAITH!

SACRIFICE MY SON! GOT IT!

WHO ARE YOU TALKING TO DADDY?

OH, NO ONE.

MORE TIME PASSED...

Um... Abraham, about that sacrifice.

RIGHT, RIGHT, I'M ON IT.

EVEN MORE TIME PASSED...

ABE! I won't say this again! sacrifice your son NOW!!

WELL, THIS IS THE FIRST I'VE HEARD OF IT.

SO WHERE ARE WE GOING?

MORAIH.

ISN'T MY BROTHER, ISHMAEL, COMING ALONG?

NO, I JUST NEED ONE OF YOU.

SO LONG! DON'T BE A STRANGER!

CALL ME, ISHMAEL!

I'M HUNGRY. WHEN WE GET WHERE WE'RE GOING, IS THERE GOING TO BE A BARBEQUE?

YOU MIGHT SAY THAT!

AND SO, ABRAHAM EXPLAINED EVERYTHING...

WHAT?!!!

WAIT! WAIT! HEAR ME OUT! IT'S NOT LIKE I'M NOT GIVING YOU A *CHOICE!*

YOU CAN EITHER *REJECT GOD* AND WALK ALL THE WAY DOWN THE MOUNTAIN, OR I CAN CARRY YOU HOME IN THIS NICE COMFY URN!

IT *IS* A LONG WALK.

I WISH WE BELONGED TO ONE OF THOSE *NON-SACRIFICING RELIGIONS.*

THAT KIND OF TALK CAN LEAD TO A PERSON *BURNING IN HELL!*

AND THERE'S ONLY *ONE WAY* TO *AVOID* THAT HORRIBLE FATE!

GET INTO THAT FIRE!

:SIGH:

OKAY, I'LL DO IT!

Abraham! You and your son have passed my test of faith! He doesn't need to jump into the fire.

GOTCHA!

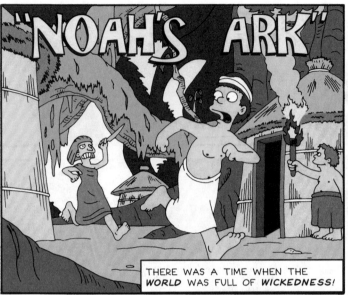

# "NOAH'S ARK"

THERE WAS A TIME WHEN THE **WORLD** WAS FULL OF **WICKEDNESS!**

FALSE IDOLS WERE WORSHIPPED...

...AND NO ONE **RECYCLED**.

GOD SPOKE TO NOAH, THE **ONLY GOOD MAN ON EARTH,** AND TOLD HIM TO BUILD AN ARK, SO HIS FAMILY WOULD BE **SPARED** FROM **THE GREAT FLOOD** TO COME.

WELL, I WAS GONNA USE ALL THIS WOOD TO MAKE A PATIO AND GAZEBO, BUT, HEY, YOU'RE THE **BOSS**!

NOAH TOLD HIS WIFE AND SONS ABOUT THE RAIN TO COME, NOT KNOWING THAT HIS NEXT DOOR NEIGHBOR WAS **EAVESDROPPING.**

SO WE'VE GOT TO START BUILDING RIGHT AWAY SHEM, HAM.

OKILLY DOKILLY, DADDYLLY-DOO!

MMM... HAM!

WAIT! WHAT WAS THAT PART ABOUT EVERYONE **DROWNING?**

SO NED'S GOT A BIG BOAT, AND ANIMALS SEEM TO LIKE HIM. IT'S NOT THE *END OF THE WORLD*.

ACTUALLY, IT *IS*.

WE ALL KNOW THE STORY SO LET'S SKIP AHEAD A MINUTE OR TWO...

I TOLD YOU WE SHOULD HAVE BEEN *NICER* TO THEM!

RAIN, RAIN GO AWAY. HAVE THE *APOCALYPSE* SOME OTHER DAY.

WHO ARE YOU *PRAYING* TO?

*GOD'S BOSS*, I GUESS.

OKAY, DON'T PANIC EVERYONE! I'VE GOT A *PLAN*!

JUST WHEN I THOUGHT WE COULDN'T GET ANY MORE *DOOMED*!

WHY YOU LITTLE...!

HOMER? THE PLAN?

⌐GAAK!⌐

OH RIGHT!

⌐COUGH!⌐

HEY! GRIFFINS!

YO! JACKALOPES!

DID YOU HEAR SOMETHING?

IT CAME FROM BEHIND THAT BUSH.

LET US GO BACK THERE AND SEE WHAT IT IS, SHALL WE?

HOW ABOUT THIS! A FLOOR ALL TO OURSELVES!

UM...DAD, ACCORDING TO THIS BLUEPRINT WE'RE ON THE *MANURE FLOOR*.

CALL IT WHAT YOU WANT, BUT IT'S DRY, AND WE'RE UNDROWNED.

WHY ARE ALL THOSE ANIMALS *SQUATTING* ON THAT GRID ABOVE US?

AAAAAAH!

FINE! SO THAT DIDN'T WORK OUT. WE'LL BE SAFE HIDDEN HERE WITH THE ANIMALS. HEY, WHERE'S LISA?

SHE'S *DEBATING* WITH THE CARNIVORES AGAIN.

ALL I'M SAYING IS THAT YOU SHOULD AT LEAST *CONSIDER* A VEGETARIAN LIFESTYLE.

I HEAR YOU, BUT WHAT PART DOES *EVOLUTIONARY BIOLOGY* PLAY IN ALL THIS?

I CAN'T TAKE THE STINK ANYMORE. I'M GOING UP ON DECK.

RIGHT BEHIND YOU!

WE CAN'T LET NOAH'S *WIFE* SEE US!

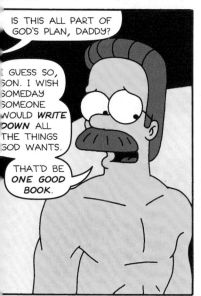

¡GASP!¡

WAY TO RAT US OUT!

I FIND THAT TERM *OFFENSIVE!*

HAVE TIME TO BE MAD.

THE FOOD'S RUN OUT, AND WE NEED TO SEND THE *PTERODACTYL* OUT TO LOOK FOR LAND.

SOMEONE *ATE* ALL THE *DINOSAURS!*

UH...YEAH, THAT'D BE ME. SORRY ABOUT THAT.

THAT DOES IT! YOU'RE GONNA MESS UP MY ARK *NEVERMORE!*

LOOK OUT, HE'S GOT A *RAVEN!*

TOO SLOW, NOAH! HAND ME THAT DOVE, BOY!

SPLAT!

HA! MISSED ME! YOU THROW LIKE A *PAGAN!*

THUD!